SO YOU WANT TO BE CAPTAIN?

Top tips from sporting heroes

Declan Gane

BLOOMSBURY
LONDON · BERLIN · NEW YORK · SYDNEY

Author's dedication

For my team – Louis, Rosa, Mariel and the real captain, Emma.

Published by Bloomsbury Publishing Plc
50 Bedford Square
London WC1B 3DP
www.bloomsbury.com

ISBN 978 1 4081 3183 1

A CIP catalogue record for this book is available from the British Library.

Cover photograph © Getty Images
Inside photographs © Getty Images
With the exception of: pp 6 courtesy of DCMS; 9 © Declan Gane; 47 © Grant Treeby/WSP; 91 © ESPN; 93

This book is produced using paper that is made from wood grown in managed, sustainable forests. It is natural, renewable and recyclable. The logging and manufacturing processes conform to the environmental regulations of the country of origin.

Designed and typeset by James Watson

Printed and bound in Croatia by Zrinski

Note

The author and publishers would like to thank all the contributors to this book. As promised a donation from the author's royalties has been made to Sport Relief. For more information on the author and the book see: www.soyouwanttobecaptain.com

Contents

Dear Louis,

I'm delighted to see you taking an interest in good captains and have this quote for you from Bobby Kennedy:

To adhere to standards, to idealism, to vision in the face of immediate dangers takes great courage and takes self-confidence. But we also know that only those who dare to fail greatly can ever achieve greatly.

Robert F. Kennedy, Day of Affirmation speech at the University of Cape Town, 6 June 1966

Hope you find this helpful.

Lord Sebastian Coe
Olympic gold medallist and Chairman of the London Organising Committee of the 2012 Olympic Games

Preface

I am delighted to lend my support for this book. At a time when we are encouraging children to be more active, *So You Want To Be Captain?* offers young people a unique insight into the world of professional sport. Inspired by contributions from an array of captains – from Rhona Martin (curling) to Michael Vaughan (cricket) – I'm sure you won't look at top-level sport in the same way.

I hope you will be inspired by some of the tips and advice on offer – and above all, have fun doing sport.

Jeremy Hunt, Culture Secretary

Foreword

I'm not really sure what I'm doing muscling in ahead of such an illustrious cast of captains and players. The nearest I ever came to being a proper footballer was having a footballer's injury. But although I wasn't the best player, I did love to play. Still do – even if it's only in the garden with my boy and his mates. So I used to do whatever it took to make myself indispensable off the pitch, knowing that they'd give me a game in the end. And that's why I have a contribution to make to this book.

In the pages that follow, you're going to meet skippers and players with all manner of strengths. They will come from a range of sports and provide a rainbow of reasons for having found themselves in charge of their dressing rooms. You'll learn a lot from them ... And you come to realise a truth, which is that there's no 'one way' to do the job.

My take on captaincy might be a little unexpected. It wasn't always about what I, as skipper, could do for the team. Instead, it was just as much about what being skipper could do for me. I'm almost ashamed to admit it, but when I was captain I saw my first responsibility as making sure that I was in that starting line-up on Sunday afternoon. So You Want To Be Captain? Well, yes. I did. And why? Because I wanted to play.

Tom Watt

Introduction

Every young player fancies him or herself as a Martin Johnson, a Kelly Holmes, a Michael Vaughan or a David Beckham. Weekend teams are full of *FECs, with mums and dads cheering them on from the sidelines.

This book was born when my own son, Louis, made it into the first XV at his secondary school. When he became captain to boot, I went to get him a book that might inspire and guide him in his new role.

There were some big thick tomes by Sir Clive Woodward, the great Mike Brearley OBE and others – but they were all for adults. So we decided to write to some captains and see what top tips they could come up with for the younger generation.

Between the two of us, we drew up a list of great captains and exceptional athletes and dropped them a line. To our surprise and delight, Gary Lineker replied almost at once. Then more and more letters began to drop onto the doormat. It soon became clear that we ought to share with others the insights and tips that these inspiring men and women were prepared to share with us – and that's when we decided to create this book.

What we have found is that captaining your team in rugby, cricket, athletics, golf, football or rowing – or high achieving at any solo sport – is down to how well you can motivate yourself and other people. A team is made up of individual players, and it's the job of a captain to inspire each and every one of them.

So flick through these words of wisdom – and next time you're facing a challenge on the field or the track, or wherever you may be, we hope you'll feel ready to take charge.

Good luck!

*Future England Captain

Declan Gane

Louis with the ball, and his sisters

Chapter 1
Get yourself ready

Prior planning and preparation prevents poor performance

Set goals

Being captain is a great experience, even though sometimes it can be a bit stressful. A captain can make or break a team, and there are many responsibilities that come with the job.

For a team to do well, captain and coach/manager must be on the same wavelength. Rule 1 is to maintain a good relationship and keep communication channels open – that means no slanging matches, especially in front of the team. But the chances are you already do get on well with everyone, otherwise you probably wouldn't be captain!

Here are a few practical pointers to remember when you're selected for captain:

- List the things you want to accomplish and describe how you want to help or improve the team. Be specific and realistic.
- List the good traits (e.g. being a good role model) and bad traits (e.g. not listening to team members) of captains you have known. You could carry this with you in your kit bag; keep it in your boot, so you are sure to glance at it every time you play.

Louis,

Be natural, composed and dedicated.

Always have short-term and long-term goals and work towards a vision of where you want your team to end up.

Don't worry about making mistakes and always try and enjoy it! This will rub off on the rest of your teammates.

Michael Vaughan OBE
England cricket captain

Michael gets his hands on the Ashes Urn on the last day of the Fifth Test in 2005.

fact file

Batsman and sometimes off-spinner, Michael began playing professional cricket aged 17, leading the England Under-19s on tour to Sri Lanka in 1993–1994 and at home against India in 1994. He played his first Test match for England in South Africa in November 1999, and was appointed captain in 2003. He captained the Ashes winning side in 2005 and is now a respected commentator.

Know the game

The laws and rules of any sport can be very complicated. As captain, you need to know the options when something out of the ordinary happens on the field. A fast decision and quick reaction to a strange set of circumstances might catch the opposition off-guard, and result in a score.

Louis,

Honesty: It is essential that you are honest both with your players and coaches. You are often the link between the players and management, so the information that you feed back can be vital for your team.

Game understanding: On the pitch, you need to have a great understanding of the laws and your team's game plan. You need to be able to make quick decisions with confidence and accuracy. If things are going wrong, you need to have the knowledge and skills to adapt.

Lead by example: I always felt it was important to lead by example. I would never ask players to do something that I was not prepared to do myself.

Approachable: As a captain, I always felt it was important to be approachable to both players and management.

Trustworthy: It's essential that players and management can trust you. Players should feel that they could talk to you with the confidence that you will not betray their trust.

Diplomacy: As a captain, I felt you should never dictate to your team off the field. It is important that decisions are shared and discussed. On the field, players should be given the responsibility for certain areas, but ultimately as a captain you make the final decision.

Inspirational: You should be able to motivate your team, not only before the game but also throughout.

Jo Yapp
Jo Yapp
England and Worcester women's rugby union captain

Jo in action during the 2004 women's rugby union International between England and Wales.

fact file

Jo made her club debut for Worcester Ladies in 1996. She joined England's elite squad in 1998, playing her first international, against Ireland, in the same year. The Worcester scrum half, who teaches physical education, captained her club side in 2003–2004, led England for the first time in the 2005 Six Nations, taking the team to the World Cup finals in 2006. Born in Shrewsbury, Jo comes from a true rugby family: she plays alongside her sister, was coached by her father, and her brother plays rugby too!

Have vision

Once you've settled on your goals, share them with your team and create a vision for the season – you might want to do better in a cup competition, aim for your side to be unbeaten all season or do the double over the local rivals. It is important for each to know what he or she is working to achieve.

Louis,

In my opinion, the greatest attributes of the best leaders are vision and example. Unless you know where you want to go, then it is hard to get there individually and collectively. A strong vision allows people to march forward towards a target, while always looking to improve and learn from the lessons life constantly offers us.

Example is paramount. A leader must lead by example in everything they do – both on and off the field. This takes discipline, hard work and sacrifice, but it is important that a leader doesn't demand of others what he/she isn't prepared to demand of themselves. My favourite philosophy is: The pain of discipline is nothing like the pain of disappointment.

Justin Langer
Middlesex and Somerset county cricket club captain

Justin with the Ashes Urn on day five of the Third Ashes Test in Perth, 2006.

fact file

Justin was a left-handed batsman best known as an Australian Test match opener and very occasionally as a wicketkeeper. He played county cricket for Middlesex (1998–2000) and was captain in 2000. He also captained the Prime Minister's XI in December 2005. Justin retired from Test cricket after the fifth Ashes Test against England on 1 January, 2007, and at the same time returned to Somerset as captain for the 2007 season. In July 2009, in his 615th innings, Justin surpassed Sir Don Bradman as Australia's leading first-class run scorer when he scored his 86th century. He hung up his boots at the end of that season.

Good loser

Knowing what it feels like to lose should spur you and your team on to win. After all, who wants to lose and see the others walk away with the medals? Stay cool, shake their hands, but don't forget that feeling of failure. Remember it when you're behind in a match so it spurs you to try harder to win.

Louis,

A captain must stay positive at all times for their team.

Good body language from a captain can give the team confidence

When the going gets tough never, ever give up.

You need to be a good loser before you can be a good winner.

A good team captain will create a winning team.

Rhona Martin MBE
Olympic curling captain

Rhona practise before the gold medal match at the Salt Lake City Winter Olympic Game Utah, 2002.

fact file

Rhona, born in Ayr, is the curler who skipped the Scotland women' team at both the European and World Championships, but is mos famous as the skip of the team that claimed the gold medal at th 2002 Olympic Winter Games.

Your game

If you're going to be captain, you need to be a pretty good player, so make sure you put in 100 per cent effort on the training ground and train harder and faster than the rest of the team. Listen to the coach, watch the pros and use what you pick up when you are on the field.

Stuart of Leeds wins the ball during the Guinness Premiership game against Saracens at Headingley Carnegie, 2007.

Louis,

Congratulations on being made captain. For me, being captain of Leeds was a huge honour. I enjoyed the role of captain and always aspired to do my best. The best piece of advice I could give you would be to concentrate firstly on yourself, your game and how you present yourself. Being a captain means that whatever you do people will follow. This is why it is so important that you set a good example, not just say the right thing.

Stuart Hooper
Leeds Tykes rugby union captain

fact file

As captain of Leeds Tykes for the 2005–2006 Guinness Premiership season, Hooper became the youngest captain in the league. Born in Devon, he could have been a league basketball player, having played at county level until he was 16, before opting for rugby union. He broke into the Saracens team while still a teenager, and while there he played alongside the French legend Abdel Benazzi in the second row. A surprise move brought him to Leeds in 2003, and in June 2005 he was called up for England 'A' against France and was part of their Churchill Cup success in Canada. 'Hoops' moved to Bath Rugby in 2008 and was named club captain for the 2011/12 season.

Early bird

Elite sportsmen will tell you it's often the small things that make the difference between winning and losing. So when you're asked by the captain to be ready on time, even if 'on time' means 5 minutes early, just do it!

Subject: So you want to be captain?

Louis,

As Ryder Cup captain in 2010 at Celtic Manor, I wanted to make sure that my team felt comfortable at all times. If they ever had a question about a decision that involved them, then they needed to know that they could speak to me about it and we would figure out a way of solving any problem.

Another element that was important to me as captain was preparation – in every aspect. I didn't want to leave any stone unturned. Even to the point that I told the players at the first team meeting that being five minutes early for a meeting was late!

Passion was also what I needed to get from my team – they had the desire to win and the ability, but they needed to have passion too.

Colin Montgomerie OBE
Ryder Cup golf captain, 2010

Colin with the Ryder Cup trophy at Celtic Manor, Wales, 2010.

fact file

Colin turned pro in 1987 and was Rookie of the Year in Europe in 1988. His consistency saw him climb the European Money List and in just five years he became Europe's No. 1, a position he held for an unprecedented seven years! Monty moved into the top 10 of the World Rankings in 1994 and was consistently ranked amongst the world's best golfers. A Ryder Cup regular, he led the Europeans from the front to a victorious win under Sam Torrance's inspired captaincy at the Belfry in 2002, and in 2004 he led from the start to finish, holing the winning putt in the Europeans' greatest triumph over the USA. By now a Ryder Cup legend, Monty describes being elected by the players to captain the 2010 Ryder Cup Team at Celtic Manor – and winning the trophy again – as the proudest achievement of his career.

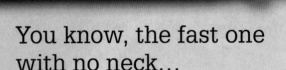

Chapter 2
Know your players

You know, the fast one
with no neck…

Put names to faces

You can't be an effective captain without knowing your team well as individual members of it, so knowing their names is a must. If you're no good at names make one up that you'll remember, but keep your nicknames polite!

At the beginning of the season, organise a non-sporting team event: a party, bowling day or anything fun that has nothing to do with training. A bonding process like this will help to build that all-important team spirit and help you to get a handle on each person. A really successful team is one that feels like an extended family; each member can count on the others and each trusts the others.

Another top tip is to stick around for a while at the end of training and after the coach's debrief. Don't be the first out of the door. Make sure you are there if anyone needs a quiet word.

Louis,

My advice to new captains is to get to know everyone's name. It really helps to build good relationships within the team. How can you motivate members of the team if you do not know their name? Likewise, if a member doesn't perform well, it helps if you can speak to him or her on first-name terms. I hope this advice is of some help and wish you and your team great success.

Tanni

Dame Tanni Grey-Thompson DBE
Paralympian athletics champion

Tanni wins at
the Athens 2004
Paralympic Games.

fact file

Tanni began her rise to fame in the 1988 Paralympic Games, competing at distances ranging from 100m to 800m. She has won 16 Paralympic medals including 11 golds, and has held over 30 world records. As a wheelchair athlete she was also the winner of five London marathons – in 1992, 1994, 1996, 1998 and 2001. Since her retirement from active competitions, Tanni continues to serve athletics as patron of the British Disabled Flying Association, working in the House of Lords and as a TV presenter in her native Wales.

Involve new players

Treat everyone the same. As long as you are fair, and you treat everyone equally, your team members will respect you. The amount of influence you have will depend on how you handle yourself, so make everyone feel equal and don't be more lenient on your mates.

Nearly everyone wants a part in decision-making, so the key is to compromise. Why not try someone else's idea? It might just be better than you thought. Give and take (on the smaller decisions), then everyone is happy.

Louis,

I always think a captain's best contribution to his team is with his performance. It's hard to tell players to do something or improve something when you're not performing at that level yourself. Also always try to talk positively. You can't change what has happened but you can influence the future!

I also believe in giving the young/new players as much of a say as everyone else in the team. By getting them involved as much as possible, you will help build their confidence and performance.

Paul Sculthorpe
St Helens and Great Britain rugby league captain

Paul scores during the 2007 Carnegie World Club Challenge match against Brisbane Broncos.

fact file

Born in Burnley, Paul started playing rugby league aged eight for Royton Tigers. He captained England Schoolboys against France and signed for Warrington aged 15. In 1998, when he moved to St Helens RLFC, he set a world record transfer fee for a forward and he was promoted to captain six years later. Paul was awarded the captaincy of Great Britain in 2005 and captained Great Britain against New Zealand in 2006. He retired in 2008.

Different characters

Whether he or she is edgy, mouthy, determined or quiet, a joker or a workman, your job as captain is to know the character of each player. You should also have a strategy for 'connecting' with them, on and off the pitch. Some will respond to gentle persuasion, others might need Sir Alex Ferguson's hairdryer treatment. Work out what delivers the best results for each team member.

Louis,

The best tip I can give is to help your players to enjoy their sport. If you enjoy what you're doing, you will usually excel at it. As a captain, you will command respect from your players if you treat them with respect. Each person in your team will be of a different character; therefore you should treat them as individuals. Before a big match, avoid negativity – keep a positive mental attitude always and never worry about what your opposition are like. Just focus on your own game. It may be a cliché, but all you can do is your best.

As captain, remember to stay calm and to enjoy yourself. If you do, then your team will follow your example.

Hope this helps.

Sam Torrance

Sam Torrance MBE OBE
Ryder Cup golf captain, 2002

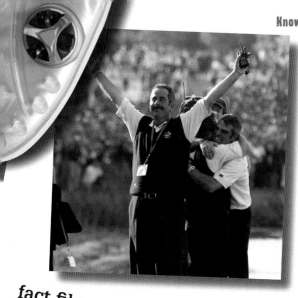

Sam celebrates
after Europe
wins the 2002
Ryder Cup.

fact file

A Scottish golfer, and one of the leading players on the European Tour from the mid-1970s to the late 1990s, Sam turned professional at 16 and joined the Euuropean Tour a year later. He achieved his first professional win in 1972 and his first European Tour win in 1976 – and went on to win 21 times. Sam played for Europe in the Ryder Cup eight times. Among his Ryder Cup highlights was sinking the winning putt in 1985, which deprived the Americans of the trophy for the first time in 28 years. Some 17 years later, Sam was the non-playing captain on the European team that won the 2002 Ryder Cup the Belfry.

Listen

'Listen to me!' 'Are you listening?' 'You'll never guess what I heard…' Listening is 50 per cent of the communication process and at least as important, if not more so, than speaking. As billionaire Google boss Eric Schmidt says: 'You don't learn very much when you yourself are talking.'

Louis,

I suppose my best tip about captaincy would be to use your ears and not get too fond of the sound of your own voice! Listening to players (whether they are speaking to you or not) can give you invaluable insights into how to get the most from them and understand what makes them tick. A captain that is forever making pronouncements and speeches can miss the one vital point – to win, you need everybody to contribute.

Hope that helps and best wishes.

Mark Butcher
England and Surrey
cricket captain

Mark in action during the third npower Test Match against New Zealand, 2002.

fact file

Mark, a left-handed batsman and occasional right-arm, medium-pace bowler, has played his entire county cricket career for Surrey, making his first-class debut in 1992. He made his Test match debut in the first Test of the 1997 Ashes series at Edgbaston and his last Test match appearance was in the first Test in South Africa in December 2004. Mark played 71 Tests, making eight centuries and captaining England once – against New Zealand in 1999. He captained Surrey from 2004 until his retirement in 2009.

Feel at ease

In any leadership role you have to get the balance right between being 'one of the gang' and being 'in charge'. This can be a tricky thing to get right, even for the pros! Try to act as naturally as possible. If you are at ease, hopefully it will rub off on to the team.

Louis,

Becoming captain of the England netball squad was a huge honour for me, but it came with a lot of duties. Not only was I responsible for my own performance, but I also had the added pressure of maintaining a harmonious and positive atmosphere within the squad.

My advice to any captain would be to get to know everyone within your team. Make them feel at ease, so they can talk to you about anything that is bothering them. You need to form a good relationship with your team and also the management and coaching staff.

My top tips are:

- motivate your team to give 100 per cent and perform to their best;
- use positive talk whether to praise or to give constructive feedback;
- be approachable to all team members.

Kate

Karen Atkinson
England netball
co-captain

Karen shields
the ball from
Australia at the
O2 Arena, 2010

fact file

During her international career as a wing attack, Karen won bronze medals at the 1998, 2002 and 2010 Commonwealth Games, as well as a silver medal with the England team at the 2010 World Netball Series in Liverpool. She captained the Hertfordshire Mavericks and also co-captained the England team, with Sonia Mkoloma, with whom she has achieved 116 caps. She retired after the World Netball Championships in Singapore in July 2011.

Chapter 3
Work for the team

There's no 'I' in team (but there's an 'M' and an 'E' if you look hard enough!)

Be a team player

Being a team does not mean that everyone has to be best friends. However, it does entail leaving any outside issues in the changing rooms and ensuring that everyone is willing to work together as a team on the field of play. The key to a good team is working together towards a common goal.

As captain, it's your job not only to be a team player yourself but also to help persuade everyone else to cooperate and work hard for the greater glory of the team.

Kelly crosses the finish line to win gold in the Women's 800 metres at the 2004 Summer Olympic Games in Athe-

Louis,

Be a team player and always want more from each player. Strive to be the best you can, and the other players will follow.

Listen to others and lead by example. Always strive for your team to do better – never settle for second best – and remember that the best time to raise your game is when you are feeling down.

Always be a leader and never give up on your dreams!

Good luck.

Dame Kelly Holmes
Olympic athletics champion

fact file

Kelly began her athletics career with Tonbridge Athletics Club at the age of 12. Aged 18, she joined the army, initially driving four-tonne trucks. However she never gave up her interest in sport, so she retrained as a PT instructor. Despite the demands of her career, she became an army judo champion. At the army athletics championships Kelly ran in the men's 1500m, rather than embarrass the women with her overriding excellence, and in one meeting she ran the 800m, the 3,000m and a relay leg in one day, winning all her races. Kelly turned pro in the early 1990s picking up lots of silver and bronze medals to go with her Commonwealth Games' golds. It was in her final major championship, the 2004 Athens Olympics where her own dreams finally came through as she stunned the world and crowned her career by winning gold in both the 800m and 1500m, bowing out as champion. Since 2009, she has been president of the Commonwealth Games England.

You can't please everyone

After your selection as captain, you will probably already have
annoyed the person who didn't get the job, so that's a great start
From now on, you need to get used to the fact that, as captain, you
will never please everybody.

Louis,

The best advice I've ever been given on captaincy, which I now
pass on to you, is this: 'You can't please everyone all the time.'
Being a captain means making often tough decisions; some of
these will be unpopular, but as long as they are well thought
through and for the benefit of the team, then you will be a
respected and successful captain.

Also, you don't have to be the best all the time. Lead by example
and attitude, but accept that others may naturally be bigger o
stronger than you. Keep striving to do better, and don't worry i
there are others in the team better than you: just always give
your best and you will gain admiration and respect.

Robin Ejsmond-Frey
Oxford University
Boating Club president

Oxford University's Robin
Ejsmond-Frey (left) on the
River Thames, 2007.

fact file

Robin was born in 1986 in Hammersmith and went to St Paul's school
in Barnes – both places being significant landmarks on the Oxford
and Cambridge Boat Race course. He read Theology at Oriel College
and was elected as Oxford's 2006–2007 Boat Race president. Robir
also played rugby union as a junior for Middlesex County.

Of benefit to all

Honesty is always the best policy, but you need to choose carefully when to tell team members a truth that may hurt. Choose a time that will benefit your teammate and the team as a whole. This may be at once, on the pitch, or it might be after the match – you decide.

Louis,

My captaincy tip is that you do not seek to be popular.

Endeavour to treat all teammates fairly and be honest with them all.

Underpinning every decision you make as a leader should be the knowledge that your decision benefits the whole team.

Will Carling OBE
England rugby union captain

Will (right) leading the England team on a lap of honour after winning the Grand Slam in 1995 against Scotland.

fact file

Will captained the England rugby team 1988–1996, winning 72 caps in all. He was the youngest-ever England captain, aged 22, and was at the time the most successful ever, seeing England to back-to-back Five Nations Grand Slam victories (1991, 1992) and to the final of the 1991 Rugby World Cup. Will also led England to a 1995 Grand Slam.

Believe and be believed

You've heard about 'managers losing the dressing-room'. Well, it'
sometimes the same for captains on the field of play, and you can
afford to let this happen. Therefore, when leading your team, mak
sure that your teammates believe in you.

Louis,

Lead by example. A good leader needs to be able to practise
what he preaches. He needs to be at his best every day. If
he/she is not, they must not show it! A great leader knows
his men and what makes the individuals tick, as well as what
different tactics may be needed to gain the best from each
team member.

A leader must believe in his troops, but, even more important,
his troops must believe in him/her.

My top tips are:

- do the job. Let your actions speak for you – 'talk is cheap';
- find a positive to every negative;
- motivate at the right times;
- listen extensively – you learn more by listening than
anything else;
- don't dictate things you can't do yourself;
- don't abuse your power or status.

Malcolm Alker
Salford City Reds rugby league captain

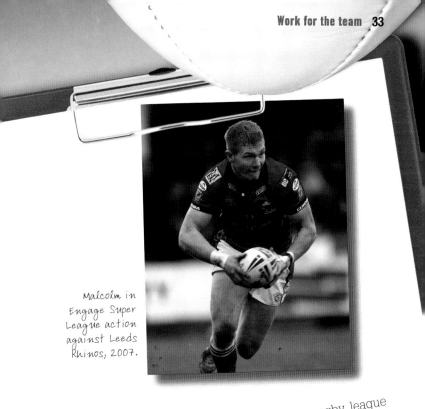

Malcolm in Engage Super League action against Leeds Rhinos, 2007.

fact file

As hooker and captain for the Salford City Reds rugby league team, Malcolm played his entire professional career at Salford and also represented Lancashire and England. A born leader, he was made captain for the fixture against Halifax at the age of 19. He retired in 2010.

Build relations

Don't allow cliques to form. Gangs of friends that won't let others in can lead to serious problems for teams that need to work together as a unit. Normally the coach will spot such a clique and try to break it up, often by 'dividing and conquering' – putting clique members in different training groups so they learn to work and respect the other team members.

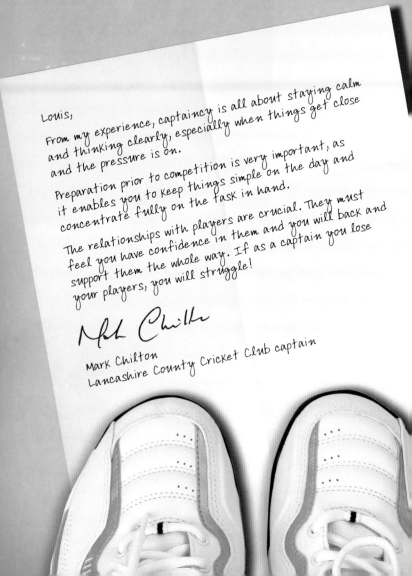

Louis,

From my experience, captaincy is all about staying calm and thinking clearly, especially when things get close and the pressure is on.

Preparation prior to competition is very important, as it enables you to keep things simple on the day and concentrate fully on the task in hand.

The relationships with players are crucial. They must feel you have confidence in them and you will back and support them the whole way. If as a captain you lose your players, you will struggle!

Mark Chilton
Lancashire County Cricket Club captain

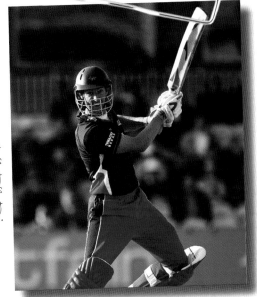

Mark edges the
ball away towards
the boundary
during a Friends
Provident Trophy
match in 2009.

fact file

Mark was promoted to Lancashire captain at the end of the 2004
season, having previously been in and out of the side since making
s debut in 1997. He played as an opening batsman and was also an
cellent slip fielder. Mark has represented England at Under-14 to
der-17 level and was awarded England Under-15 Batsman of the
r in 1992. He retired at the end of 2011 after Lancashire took the
ty championship for the first time in 77 years.

Care about the group

Most teams meet at least twice a week, so the chances are that you
are with good friends and make good friends. As a captain it's your job
to care about the group as a whole as well as its individual members.

Louis,

Be honest. What is your reason for what you do? You have
to be passionate about what you do – it all starts at the
top. Most of all, you have to care about the group you lead.

Tom Lehman
Ryder Cup captain, 2006

Tiger Woods
chats to USA
team captain Tom
Lehman (right)
at the 2006
Ryder Cup at
the K Club.

fact file

Tom was born in Austin, Minnesota, attended the University of Minnesota, where he studied business/accounting, and turned golf professional in 1982. After a slow start he regained his PGA Tour card in 1992 and was named PGA Tour Player of the Year in 1996, having just experienced the highlight of his career – victory in the 1996 British Open. Some 10 years later, Tom captained the US Ryder up team at the K-Club in Ireland.

Don't go changing

Be yourself, the self you were before you gained the captaincy. Your character was part of the reason you were promoted to captain, so stay true to yourself.

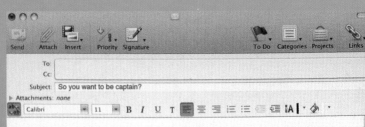

Louis,

Lead from the front. No one expects you to be the best at everything, but do what you can do to the best of your ability with the maximum enthusiasm and determination.

Also, be honest. Don't change your personality because someone has given you responsibility. When tough decisions need to be made, don't take the easy option or tell a convenient half-truth – say it how it is. You need to earn respect, not demand it.

Martin Corry
England and Leicester Rugby Football Club captain

Barbarians captain Martin runs at the England lines during the International Friendly match at Twickenham, 2009.

fact file

Martin captained Leicester Tigers to three grand finals and lifted the Guinness Premiership and EDF Energy Cup, a first Double in the professional era. The following year he captained England in the crucial pool games during his third Rugby World Cup, in 2007, leading a team that had been written off by everyone through the knockout stages. England went on to beat Australia in the quarter-finals and France in the semi-finals, before losing a tight final to South Africa. Martin won 64 caps for England and toured Australia and New Zealand with the British and Irish Lions.

Individuals need a team

In a solo sport you're rather like all members of a team rolled into one person, including the captain, although there is always support behind you, even if it's just Mum, driving you to the fixture. Your character will determine what style of captaincy is most suitable for you. Some solo-sport stars such as Michael Schumacher and Andy Murray call all the shots, whereas others will be more open to well guided, practical advice from experienced coaches.

Louis,

Despite ski racing being deemed an individual sport, you can succeed only if you have a great team behind you. Every team needs a leader. For me my leader has always been my coach, who is someone I respect, someone who can command the attention of a room, and is someone who is not afraid to delegate. Yet when I need my coach, he is always there to listen. The biggest thing a leader contributes to me and my sport is that he or she instils the confidence in me to go out there and do my best. My coach helps me to manage my expectations and realise my goals.

Chemmy Alcott
Great Britain No. 1 ski racer

Chemmy clears a gate at the Women's Vancouver 2010 Winter Olympics Giant slalom event.

fact file

Chemmy was the first British skier to win a run in a World Cup race (Soelden, giant slalom), became the first British woman to qualify for and race in the World Cup finals and the first also to win the British Land National Championships for the sixth time in a row. A four-year climb has seen her move up the World Rankings, in which she finished the 2010 season ranked eighth in the Supercombined, was in the top 20 in super G and in the world's top 30 in three disciplines.

Chapter 4
The field of play

Follow me, men!

Actions speak louder

Napoleon is supposed to have said: 'a picture is worth a thousand words' on the battlefield, and it's the same on the playing field. Seeing a captain getting stuck-in and actually getting on with whatever needs to be done is a great way to demonstrate to team members exacting what is required.

Google ex-England football captain, Terry Butcher – he looked like he'd been in a battle when he led the team in the World Cup qualifier against Sweden. His captaincy in the 1990 campaign saw England qualify without conceding a single goal.

Louis,

I think the best way to be a captain is to try and lead by example. A straight, tough action or play in a game will speak a thousand times louder and mean much more to your teammates than any long speech.

Try to be as honest as possible at all times with yourself and your teammates.

Work out which personalities in your team respond to encouragement, which to being berated and shouted at.

Most importantly, enjoy the game and being captain.

Jamie Peacock
Great Britain rugby league captain

Jamie on the attack during the Engage Super League match against Bradford Bulls, 2009.

fact file

A product of the Bradford Bulls junior programme, Jamie was voted Player's Player and the Man of Steel in 2003 and was the only British player named in the 2006 World XIII. Jamie was recognised as one of the best back-row forwards in the world, and he was promoted to Great Britain captain for the 2006 Tri Nations Series. In 2007 he captained the side to a series whitewash over New Zealand, confirming his status as one of the best players of his generation.

Lead by example

Leadership isn't all about blood and gore, and 'go get 'em'. It is more subtle than that. Your own approach to the game, the ref and the opposition, and how you handle yourself during and after the game will have a great influence on your team.

Louis,

I have come across two major types of captains during my rugby league career. There are those who lead through words, by providing direction, and those who lead by example. Both types of captainship are equally effective provided the captain has gained the respect of his or her fellow teammates and demonstrated who is the true leader.

My own captaincy style is to lead by example on the field. Off the field I give plenty of encouragement during training and try to be approachable so a player can talk to me if he or she is experiencing problems.

A captain must be professional in the way they view the game as the younger players look towards the captain as somewhat of a role model.

Richard Swain
Hull rugby league captain

Richard in action for Hull FC at the KC Stadium, 2006.

fact file

Richard played for the Hunter Mariners, Melbourne Storm, Brisbane Broncos and for the New Zealand national side. The former Kiwi hooker captained Hull FC for three seasons, leading them to two major finals and lifting the 2005 Challenge Cup. Injury forced his retirement in 2007.

Front man

'When the going gets tough, the tough get going', as the old saying goes. This is when teams most need their captains to give that extra little bit of inspiration, which really fires the rest of them.

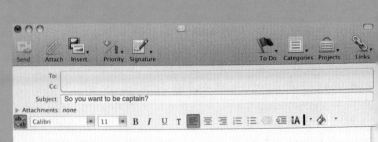

Louis,

I believe the best captains are the ones who lead from the front on the pitch. I always looked to do this and not allow things away from the field to take too much away from what is really important. When it comes to the crunch, people want to see you leading your team in a way that inspires others.

Honesty and sincerity with your teammates mean so much. I always liked to set small, realistic goals, so they were achieved more often, thus often breeding confidence. Any setbacks were therefore small and reversible.

I was never one for too many words before a game. There is a time and place to motivate people, and saving this for the key moments gives more impact. It is important to recognise the occasion and scope of what you are achieving or about to achieve. I would praise where praise is due, raise issues that need to be raised; but never overdo it. I always see over celebration or praise as a sign of thinking that something was not expected or believed possible.

I would always say to aspiring captains that they should never ask of people what they would not do themselves. Lead from the front and choose your words and actions carefully – timing is everything!

Ben Hawes
Great Britain and England hockey captain

Ben in GB action at the Beijing Olympic Green Hockey Stadium, 2008.

fact file

Ben made his international debut at the 2002 Commonwealth Games in Manchester and went on to captain the Great Britain side to take gold in the Olympic qualifiers in Chile. He also scored in the opening 1 win over Egypt at the 2004 Olympics Games, in Athens. Ben captained the team again in the 2008 Olympic Games, in Beijing, and won gold with England at the 2009 Euro Hockey Championships.

Dig deep

Love them or hate them, Manchester United is a team that neve[r] gives up. When 2–0 down with 10 minutes to play, United players stil[l] believe they will score three – and win. As a captain on the field, it'[s] your job to get everyone to believe and dig deep.

Louis,

Lead by example on the pitch and have high standards on and off the field. Be a calming influence when everybody around you could be losing it. Dig deep when things are going against you – be mentally tough and physically tough. Being a good motivator and knowing who to console, who to have a dig at, is key.

Andy Todd
Blackburn Football Club captain

fact file

Andy is a central defender who can play at full-back or as a defensive midfielder. Son of former Derby County and England defender Colin Todd, Andy made his debut with Middlesbrough and was loaned to Swindon Town before joining Bolton Wanderers in 1995. He won the 1996–1997 Division One Championship with Bolton and made his way via Charlton Athletic and Grimsby Town to Blackburn in 2002. Mark Hughes gave him the Blackburn captain's armband in 2004.

...dy in action during the ...rclays Premiership match against Sunderland at Ewood Park, 2006.

Mix it up

The manager will make the big calls, but as captain you are his representative on the pitch so you get to call the shots there. If the usual practice-ground moves aren't working, why not try something different?

Louis,

I always try to lead by actions on the field and am always willing to give advice!

You have to stay positive, even when things don't go your way.

If you always do what you have always done, you will always get what you deserve.

Lee Briers
Wales and Warrington Wolves rugby league captain

Lee with the ball against Salford Reds at the Millennium Stadium, Cardiff, 2007.

fact file

As a rugby league stand-off, Lee Briers captained St Helens before joining Warrington Wolves, where he holds the record for most points scored in a match (40 from 14 goals and three tries) and most goals in a match (14). These were both recorded in the 2000 Challenge Cup against York. Lee stepped down as Wolves captain in 2007. He has also captained Wales.

R-E-S-P-E-C-T

Although it may be considered a bit old-fashioned, many of the best professional players and captains in the world base their games on respecting others. At amateur level, there is no excuse at all for any lack of respect.

Louis,

For me, rugby is based on enjoyment and respect. If you have the respect of your team and coaches, and in turn you respect them, then you will enjoy the game – and, after all, that's why we play!

Bob Casey
London Irish rugby union captain

Bob in action during the Guinness Premiership match between London Irish and Sale Sharks at the Madejski Stadium, 2010.

act file

ob has represented Ireland at Schools, Under-19, Under-21, Ireland
'A' and Under-25 levels and won his first full cap in 2000 – the year after
oining Leinster. He moved to London Irish in July 2002 becoming the
Club's 2003–2004 Players' Player of the Season and was the 2004–2005
London Irish Supporters Club Player of the Season. Bob captained the
Exiles to a Heineken Cup semi-final with Toulouse in 2008 and led
them to the Guinness Premiership final in 2009.

Chapter 5
Not according to the plan

Mistakes happen, deal with it

Always smile

There should always be a game plan of some sort. How detailed it is will depend on your playing level. However, one fact is guaranteed – the game will never pan out totally as you have planned it. After all, it's the opposition's job to try and spoil things!

So what is Plan B or Plan C? If alternative strategies and tactics, depending on what has happened, were discussed before the match or at half time, the options should be there. So if things start to go wrong and mistakes are made, your job as a good captain is to ensure the team puts these behind them and moves on. This can often be hard to do, yet what's done is done. Be positive, decisive and think forward, not back.

As captain, it's your job also to make sure there are no recriminations

Louis,

To be a good captain doesn't necessarily mean you have to be the best player in the team. The thing that counts is that you have the respect of your teammates, by showing them respect.

The tactical aspect requires you to make the right decision at the right time for the good of the team. If you do make a mistake, it is essential that you get your next decision correct.

Enjoyment is a big part of captaining. Don't make it a burden - and always smile.

Matthew Burke

Matthew Burke
Australia and Newcastle Falcons rugby union captain

Matt successfully kicks and converts Ben Tune's try at the 1999 Rugby World Cup Final, Cardiff.

fact file

One of the greatest full-backs of all time, Matthew was a national hero down under after kicking the Wallabies to the 1999 Rugby World Cup in Wales. He scored a remarkable 24 points against South Africa in the semi-final, and then bettered it with 25 against France in the final. A magnificent, 10-year international career has seen Matt rack up 81 caps and score 878 points – the fifth highest of all time when he retired from Test rugby in June 2004. His superb leadership won him the 2005–2006 Falcons Player of the Season Award and the captaincy for the 2006–2007 campaign.

Be your own person

Picture your team with the trophy on the podium after the match, and keep that image in your head. You have to be confident at all times – even if a decision you make turns out not to have been for the best.

Louis,

Be your own person and make your own mistakes. You cannot captain by committee, ie, taking advice from everyone. You choose a couple of players to discuss cricketing decisions with, but then make your own mind up. Be honest with your players – don't 'flannel' them. Be positive and quietly confident.

Geoffrey Boycott OBE
England and Yorkshire cricket captain

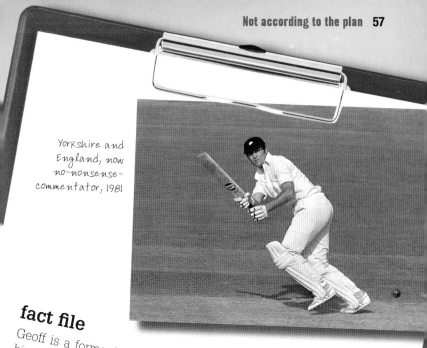

Yorkshire and
England, now
no-nonsense-
commentator, 1981

fact file

Geoff is a former Yorkshire and England cricketer who established
himself as one of England's finest opening batsmen. He began
playing for his home county in 1962, and only two years later played
in his first Test against Australia. Over the next 18 years he scored
8114 runs in 108 Test matches. He was the first England cricketer to
pass 8000 Test runs, and is still England's fourth all-time run scorer.
Geoff captained England twice in 1978, and following his retirement
in 1986 has become an often outspoken cricket commentator on both
radio and television.

Encourage

It is important to know the character of each team member. Then when someone makes a mistake, you should be able to encourage them in a way that will motivate them. Some players will want an arm around their shoulder, but with others you will be able to take the mickey out of them for the rest of the season, which will spur them on.

Louis,

As a captain I have always tried to lead by example, by demonstrating a good attitude, good discipline and a 100 per cent work-rate all the time.

I tend to encourage players as much as possible. Everyone makes mistakes, and people don't need to be shouted at all the time!

Matt Holland
Charlton Athletic football captain

Matt celebrates scoring Ireland's equaliser against Cameroon at the 2002 World Cup finals.

fact file

Rejected by Arsenal for being 'too small', Matt joined the West Ham United academy but never played for the first team. He transferred to Bournemouth, in 1995, where he played 116 games and was promoted to captain. Two years later he signed for Ipswich Town, where he became a crowd favourite and again achieved the captain's armband. Whilst with the Tractor Boys, Matt captained the club into the Premier League and then into Europe before the team was relegated in 2002. On his return from the 2002 World Cup with Ireland, Matt turned down an offer from Aston Villa, but 10 months later he made the move to Charlton, where he again assumed the captain's armband.

Enjoy

Let's face it, turning out to play at 10 a.m. on a cold, dark, rain
January morning is not always very inviting, so you have to enjoy it
Don't let whatever you do for pleasure become a chore. Make it fu
for you and all.

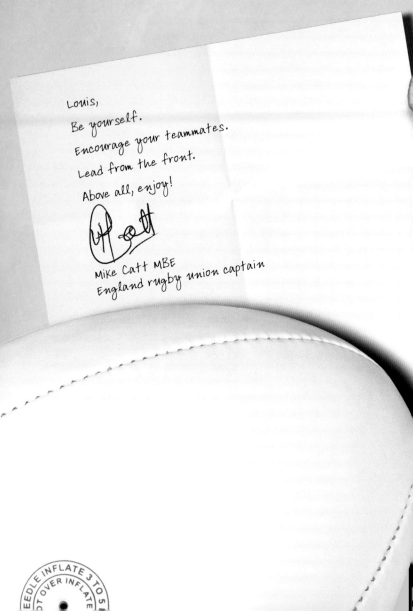

Louis,

Be yourself.

Encourage your teammates.

Lead from the front.

Above all, enjoy!

Mike Catt MBE
England rugby union captain

France's captain Raphael Ibanez (centre) tries to tackle Mike (front) during the VI Nations at Twickenham, 2007.

fact file

South African-born Mike had trials with Gloucester RFC before making his debut as a 21-year-old fly-half for Bath in 1992. He made his international debut against Wales in 1994, was part of England's Grand Slam winning side the following year and played in the 1995 Rugby World Cup. Mike then played in the final Test of the 1997 British and Irish Lions Tour to South Africa. Following considerable success with Bath, he joined London Irish in 2004 and helped them secure European Cup qualification. Mike came out of retirement to captain England against Wales in the 2007 RBS Six Nations.

Don't worry

'It's only a game!' Sometimes you might not want to hear those words, but it really is only a game. So while it is important to want to do well, to work hard and to do your best, you shouldn't let any situation upset you.

Louis,

It's the captain's job to create belief, confidence and togetherness throughout the team and you can do this by:

- demonstrating your own commitment;
- leading by example;
- listening to your team;
- being the best you can;
- not worrying or being afraid of defeat, which is part of any sport.

Andy Griffin
Stoke City Football Club captain

Andy in action during the Coca Cola Championship match against Watford at Vicarage Road, 2008.

fact file

Andy began his career at Stoke City, where he established a reputation as a solid wing-back defender. Having attracted the attention of Sir Bobby Robson, Andy moved to Newcastle in 1998. In the 2002–2003 UEFA Champions League, he rekindled his side's campaign by scoring the winning goal against Juventus. After spells at Portsmouth and Derby County, Andy returned to Stoke in 2008 and within three weeks was made captain.

Chapter 6
The big unwind

Life off the field

Off-field understanding

A football match is 90 minutes long, rugby is 80 minutes and netba[ll]
60. A round of golf might last a few hours, and cricket can go on for fiv[e]
days. However, for most young players, the chances are that they wi[ll]
actually spend more time together off the field than on it. So whethe[r]
it's on the coach, in the changing room, in the clubhouse or at schoo[l]
there will be plenty of time for a captain to get a real understanding [of]
his or her teammates. You should see what motivates them and how
they learn best. Then use this knowledge to develop their playing skills[.]

Louis,

Get to know all your players off the field as much as
possible. This makes you better at knowing what to say
to them and when to say it. Everyone is different so
you will have to think about how best to communicate
with them. Keep your ears open and your mouth closed
to pick up all these clues.

Jeremy Snape
Leicestershire County Cricket Club captain

Jeremy in action at the Twenty20 Cup against Derbyshire, County Ground, 2007.

fact file

Jeremy, a right-handed batsman and right-arm, off-break bowler, began his career in 1991 at Northamptonshire, which won the NatWest Trophy in his first season at the club. He moved to Gloucestershire for the 1999 season and was part of the treble-winning side of 2000, making his one-day international (ODI) debut for England against Zimbabwe in 2001–2002 and winning the Man of the Match Award in his first game. Jeremy played nine more ODIs over the next year. He also left Gloucestershire at the end of the 2002 season and signed for Leicestershire. Jeremy was part of the Leicestershire side that won the Twenty20 Cup in August 2004. He was appointed captain two years later and retired in 2008.

Honesty, the best policy

Don't talk rubbish – just say it as it is. Remember, a lie gets half way around the world before the truth has a chance to put its pants on!

Louis,

Leadership is about giving your all in everything you do – not just on the field, in the gym or on the track, but also in life itself.

Honesty is very important. If you are honest with yourself, you can be honest with your teammates.

Finally, enjoy being captain. There will be ups and downs – highs and lows – but they all help to make you a better person.

Keep smiling.

Kevin Sinfield
Leeds Rhinos rugby league captain

Kevin in
action during
the Engage
Super League
match against
Bradford
Bulls at the
Millennium
Stadium, 2011.

fact file

Kevin was recognised early on as an extremely special player. He joined the Rhinos in 1996, making his debut at 16. He was promoted to the captaincy in 2003, having become a first-choice regular at the club as he was able to play at loose-forward or stand-off. He is also an astute goal kicker and has amassed over 500 points in just five seasons. In 2005, Kevin became the first Leeds captain ever to lift the World Club Challenge Trophy, and he led his side back to the Powergen Challenge Cup and grand final. In 2009, Kevin led his team to victory in a third successive grand final, becoming the first player in history to captain four championship-winning teams.

Be good!

It's tricky telling people what to do, then failing to do it yourself. Getting yellow or red cards; incurring a fine or a ban – these don't do you or your team any favours at all, and you'll lose the respect of your teammates. Being a captain means being good, stepping up to the mark and showing everyone how it's done.

Louis,

Always call 'heads' when you toss up.

Lead by example, especially in terms of your behaviour.

Enjoy the game!

Gary Lineker OBE
England football captain

Gary celebrates with the equaliser against West Germany in the 1990 World Cup Semi-Final in Turin. West Germany won on penalties.

fact file

Born in Leicester, Gary excelled as a sportsman from a young age. He began his career as an apprentice with his home-town club and played for Everton, Barcelona and Tottenham Hotspur before ending his career with the Japanese club Grampus Eight. Never once, in his entire career, did he receive a red or yellow card. He is now a well-known football commentator.

Never stop learning

Lifelong learning is key to success in everything. So by pitching yourself against better teams and better captains you will pick up tips and ways of doing things that will improve your game and leadership. It might not be cool to talk about, but the best people never stop learning.

Louis,

Here are a few pointers that I believe are particularly important:

- never stop learning;
- be true to yourself as well as your teammates;
- never ask them to do something that you wouldn't do yourself;
- encourage teammates at all times;
- be positive – not negative;
- enjoy yourself and celebrate success – remember it will end one day!

Gavin Hastings OBE
Scotland and British and Irish Lions rugby union captain

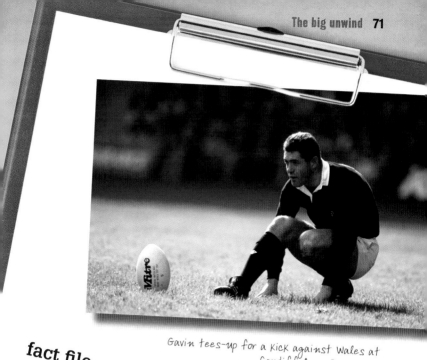

Gavin tees-up for a kick against Wales at Cardiff Arms Park, 1992.

fact file

'Big Gav' is one of the best rugby players to come out of Scotland. He played for Watsonians, London Scottish, Cambridge University, Scotland and the British and Irish Lions, and was one of the outstanding players of his generation, winning 61 caps for Scotland, 20 as captain. He played full-back and captained the Lions on the tour to New Zealand in 1993.

Community worker

A great way to consolidate your own skills is to pass them on to others. Helping out in training younger teams and explaining things to them will make it easier for you to understand what you are doing yourself. Strange but true – it really works.

Louis,

If you've been made captain then you should be really proud and realise that, without being too big-headed, you are seen as an outstanding player and you are also very well thought of as a person. At such a young age, I'm sure you will be extra proud to know that you are the one that some of the young players will be looking up to in all-important matches and winning situations.

At your age it should be all about having fun and hopefully lifting a few trophies!! In professional sport, captaincy comes with added responsibilities on and off the pitch. You need to set a good example both on the pitch and also with the media. You should get out into the community and give time to share your skills with others. We do this at Bolton Wanderers which really helps to build your name and reputation as well as that of a great club.

Kevin Davies
Bolton Wanderers football captain

Kevin in action against Newcastle United at the Reebok Stadium, Bolton, 2010.

fact file

Kevin played as a schoolboy with Sheffield United, breaking into the first team at Chesterfield in 1993. A hat-trick on the way to the semi-finals of the 1997 FA Cup brought Kevin to the attention of Southampton, where he stayed until 2003, having spent the 1998–1999 season with Blackburn Rovers. But it was with Bolton Wanderers where he rediscovered his best form, ending his first season by winning the club's Player of the Year Award. Kevin became captain on 31 January 2009 scoring two goals in Bolton's 3–2 victory over Tottenham Hotspur, equalling his record for goals in a Premier League season. In 2010, at the age of 33, he made his debut for England at Wembley.

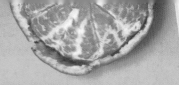

Go the extra mile

You don't get to be a captain without being dedicated to your sport and your team, so you probably already put in 110 per cent. But, like all elite athletes, the best captains simply work harder than everyone else, on every aspect of their game. It's an honour to be captain, but with it comes responsibilities that mean extra work!

To:

Cc:

Subject: So you want to be captain?

Attachments: none

Louis,

The three most important qualities in a good captain are leadership, commitment and being willing to put the team first. If those around you can see that you're applying yourself in the correct manner with regards to all three of those qualities, then you're doing your job as a captain.

You must always remember that as the captain you have an extra responsibility. On the pitch, you can be the voice of the manager and you are a bit more aware of other players' performances. You're not just responsible for yourself. Off the pitch, you just have to represent the football club as best you can – but I think all professionals should be aware of that anyway. Being captain means you probably get a bit more involved in the organisation of any off-the-field activities.

Bryan Robson was my hero when I was growing up. He was everything you want your captain to be. He would lead by example and he would always be the first to 'go the extra mile'. All the players at Manchester United respected him enormously because he was a natural leader on and off the pitch.

Phil Neville

Everton captain and England player

Phil celebrates scoring the second goal at Molineux during the 2011 Barclays Premier League match against Wolves.

fact file

Phil began his career at Manchester United alongside older brother Gary and a bunch of other hopefuls that included David Beckham, Ryan Giggs and Paul Scholes. While at Old Trafford, Phil helped to win six Premier League titles, three FA Cups and the European Cup. In 2005 he moved to Everton, making his Premier League debut for the Toffees against United, the first time he and Gary had played for opposing teams. Phil's attitude, work-rate and willingness to play anywhere saw him confirmed as vice-captain in 2006 and as club captain a year later. As an International, Phil was the youngest member of Terry Venables' squad for Euro 1996, and a regular first-choice player as a left-back under Kevin Keegan. He won 59 caps.

Chapter 7
Captain Sensible

Look into my eyes

A degree in people

Psychology is the science of mind and behaviour, and as we've already seen captaincy is probably more to do with how you can deal with and get the best out of your teammates than actually playing the game – but of course that is pretty important too.

Many really great players can be boisterous and fiery, unpredictable and short-tempered, so keeping calm and knowing what makes any player tick is really what it's all about.

Louis,

I was fortunate to play under some great captains during my time as an England player – Gooch, Gatting, Gower, Willis to name a few – but two captains who I believe influenced my career more than any were Brian Close and Mike Brearley.

Closey led by example, never asking you to do anything he hadn't done himself. His self-belief and will to win were instilled in me from day one.

Mike Brearley was simply the best. As Rodney Hogg once said: 'Brears – he has a degree in people.' He knew how to get the best out of me and of my teammates, understanding what made the individual tick.

Sir Ian Botham OBE
England and Somerset cricket captain

Ian bowls during the Fifth Ashes Test against Australia at Old Trafford, 1981.

fact file

Sir I.T. Botham was not only the top English cricketer of the 1980s but also the leading sports personality of the era. Just a year after being elevated from Somerset to his England debut in 1977, he was undisputed as the country's leading all-rounder and was promoted to captain within three years. In 1981 came the most famous few weeks in English cricket history, when Sir Ian (under Mike Brearley's captaincy) led England to an astonishing Ashes victory with three performances two with bat, one with ball – of mystical brilliance. These victories caused a boom in support for English cricket that reverberated through the decade. Sir Ian remained an international cricketer until 1992 and is now a well-respected commentator on the game.

Step up

Being there when you're needed is a key part of the captain's role.
If things kick off and threaten to turn nasty, be there to calm things
down. Before that, if you see a situation developing between two
opposing players, speak to your teammate and alert the ref. Captains
should always be proactive.

Louis,

There is no correct way to be a captain. You have to do
what comes naturally to you. By this I mean try not to
copy other people – instead, find a technique that best
suits your attributes.

The one thing that you must do is to train and play to
the best of your ability. Do not ask anyone to do what
you would not do yourself. You must set an example with
your work ethic on and off the field.

Another huge job for a captain, which set Martin Johnson
out from other captains, is to step to the front and lead
by actions when the game is not going the way of your
team. Always promote yourself when your team needs you.

Hugh Vyvyan
England and Saracens rugby union captain

Hugh controls a line-out during the Premiership match against London Wasps at Vicarage Road, 2009

fact file

Hugh, as a no.8 and sometimes lock-forward, has led Newcastle Falcons as well as captaining the England 'A' squad on two Churchill Cup Tours. In 2002, he toured with the full England side and in 2004 captained the Falcons when they won the Powergen Cup for a second time. Hugh then joined Saracens, where he was made captain before even having played a game! He is the most capped Premiership player.

Knit it all together

There's loads to do as a captain, which is why sometimes even really good players have a drop in form when promoted to the captaincy. It's a tough job to keep playing well as an individual while remembering and carrying out all of the captain's duties. So KISS – **K**eep **I**t **S**imple **S**tupid. Do the basics and build on those game by game. Get to a point where you're confident with what you've done before trying out new things.

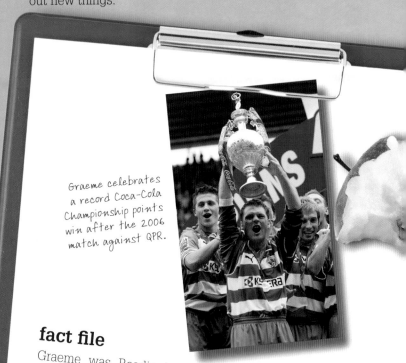

Graeme celebrates a record Coca-Cola Championship points win after the 2006 match against QPR.

fact file

Graeme was Reading's captain, right-back and longest-serving player, having signed for the club from York City in the summer of 1998 for £700,000. He began his career as a trainee with City in 1991 and went on to play more than 120 games for the Minstermen. His first few seasons for Reading were hampered by injury but he quickly became an integral part of the team, and when Phil Parkinson left the club in 2003 Graeme served as club captain until he left to join Southampton in 2009. Born in Middlesbrough, he qualifies to play for Scotland through his family and has been capped four times – his first Scotland cap being against Wales in 2004.

Louis,

Do:

- be yourself;
- praise;
- lead by example;
- set high standards;
- encourage people to accept responsibility.

Don't:

- try to do everyone's job;
- make excuses if things go wrong;
- let your head go down;
- forget those not in the starting line-up!

Always remember that people will be looking to you, so your body language is key! At all times, look as though you are completely in control and calm, even if you're not inside. Players can draw so much strength from their captain, but it can be the opposite if they get the wrong message from you.

An effective captain should also take individual player's character into consideration. Some players respond well if you talk calmly to them privately, but will go to pieces if confronted in an aggressive, public manner. With others, you need to be 'at them' constantly for their performance levels to be maximised. Knowing the difference is vital.

Taking all these things into consideration, Phil Parkinson would be the best captain I have played under. He was able to knit diverse characters into a coherent, effective team, whilst also ensuring that he was always a positive figure on the pitch and in the dressing-room merely by the way he conducted himself.

Graeme Murty
Reading Football Club captain and Scotland player

It's an honour

There's no doubt that being selected as captain is a great honour, so you should firstly be very pleased and proud that your contribution to the team has been recognised. Then, after 10 seconds, get back to work and don't let the new position go to your head!

Louis,

Being captain of a team is always an honour, especially when you have worked hard for years to get there.

If I could offer any advice, it would be to set an example to your teammates through your commitment and conduct.

The most influential captain I have played under would be Matt Jackson. He is a great leader and someone all players in our dressing-room look up to because he sets great examples both on and off the pitch.

Leighton Baines
Wigan Athletic and Everton football captain and England player

Leighton fights for the ball with Javier Hernandez during the International Friendly against Mexico at Wembley, 2010.

fact file

As a highly promising, young defender, Liverpudlian Leighton rose through the ranks at Wigan to command the left-back position. He became a first-team regular in 2003–2004 and was named the club's Young Player of the Year. Leighton is a composed player going forward, and he has a tremendous left foot. His ability earned him a first call-up to the England Under-21s for the game against Austria in September 2004. In 2007 a £6 million transfer saw him move to Everton, which he captained for the first time in a UEFA Europa League match two years later. Leighton made his full England debut against Egypt in March 2010.

Actions speak louder than words

You don't like it and your teammates know you don't like it, but by excelling in areas that you find challenging you will set a great example for the rest of the team to follow. It's not rocket science – more mind over matter.

Louis,

Being a captain is one of the greatest honours – if not the greatest honour – an individual can achieve within a team sport. This is because that person has not only shown an ability to perform to an acceptable level as a player but is also highly regarded as a person by his fellow players and coaches.

The best piece of advice I've been given is to ensure that, first and foremost as a captain, you lead by example both on and off the pitch by the way you act and conduct yourself. This includes having a positive attitude in training (even if it's a drill you don't like!!) and in games, as well as showing respect and eagerness to learn from both your coaches and referees. Such an approach will rub off on your teammates (do not underestimate how much effect your actions have on your teammates, even if they don't show it!).

The best words I can give you is to savour every moment, approach each decision with a cool and collected head and remember sometimes you have to hate to lose, more than you love to win!

Rory Best
Ireland and Ulster rugby union captain

Rory passes the ball during the Test match against the All Blacks at Aviva Stadium, 2010.

fact file

Rory captained Belfast Harlequins in 2002 and joined Ulster two years later. He made his debut as a replacement at home to Munster in 2005 – the same year he made his international debut for Ireland (also as a replacement) against the mighty All Blacks. Rory replaced his brother Simon as captain of Ulster in 2007 and captained the Ireland team that toured North America in 2009.

The list is long

With so much to remember as captain it's surprising you can play at all. But, as we saw at the start, you've been selected because you're probably doing a lot of good things already without even thinking. That's the trick you have to master. Golfer Gary Player summed it all up when he said: 'The harder I practise, the luckier I get!' You do need natural ability, but there are always things to learn and practise.

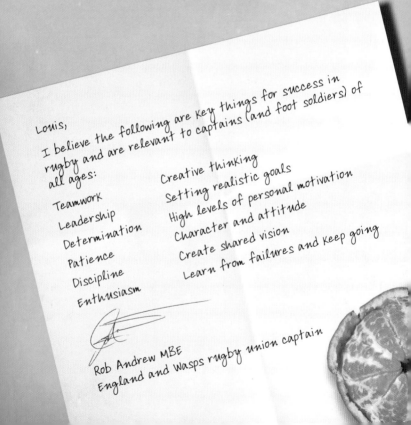

Louis,

I believe the following are key things for success in rugby and are relevant to captains (and foot soldiers) of all ages:

Teamwork
Leadership
Determination
Patience
Discipline
Enthusiasm

Creative thinking
Setting realistic goals
High levels of personal motivation
Character and attitude
Create shared vision
Learn from failures and keep going

Rob Andrew MBE
England and Wasps rugby union captain

Rob passes the ball during a friendly match against the Soviet Union at Twickenham, 1991.

fact file

In 1981, Rob was captain of the 1st XV at Barnard Castle School and went on to captain Cambridge University in the 1985 Varsity match. He joined Wasps RFC in the 1980s, winning the English League in 1990, and he played in the Rugby World Cup in 1991 and 1995. During a 12-year international career, Rob became England's leading points-scorer with 396 in 71 appearances, and he is considered as one of the greatest fly-halves in rugby. Rob joined Newcastle Gosforth in 1995, becoming coach as Newcastle Falcons joined the professional era. Rob is credited with discovering Jonny Wilkinson. He is now the Rugby Football Union's director of operations.

Chapter 8
Seen it all before, have you?

Commentators tell it like it is

Say thank you

It really does happen throughout rugby. Using 'please' and 'thank you' and calling the ref 'sir' make for a civilized and much more enjoyable game.

Louis,

- Lead by example – don't ask your team to do anything you are not prepared to do yourself;
- Listen as well as talk – team members can input invaluable advice;
- Be inclusive – try to make sure everyone feels part of the team;
- Be open and honest – even with difficult issues players will accept that you acted out of the best motives;
- Don't ignore the small things – you will be amazed how a small 'thank you' or similar will be appreciated;
- Plan and prepare – don't leave things to chance.

Brian Moore

England and British and Irish Lions, Nottingham, Harlequins, Richmond rugby union captain

Brian directs play during the England vs. All Blacks game at Twickenham, 1993 England won the match 15-9.

fact file

Brian 'Pit Bull' Moore made his name playing at Harlequins and represented England 64 times between 1987 and 1995. He played in three Rugby World Cups and was also a member of the England side that won Grand Slams in 1991, 1992 and 1995. Brian was voted 1991 Rugby World Player of the Year. He toured twice with the British and Irish Lions, and gained five Test caps. A lawyer by profession, Brian is also a qualified referee as well as a popular BBC commentator.

The odd white lie

All captains should be optimists and inspire optimism in their sides.
If that might be bending the truth a little to spread confidence, then
that's acceptable, isn't it? Call it kidology.

Louis,

One of my heroes is Ian Turnick, who was the skipper of a
'social' rugby union team representing Caldy Rugby Club
on the Wirral. He showed great leadership in regularly
getting a team of unfit wasters on to the pitch. He
showed great sense in not pushing too hard, using a light
touch and humour, reminding players to do justice to
themselves and the team, fabricating the odd white lie
about the strength of the opposition in order to motivate,
while leading by example and charging at every opponent.

Turnick's 'Tornados', as they were nicknamed, were writing
cheques their bodies couldn't cash, but win or lose it was a
great time and the skipper deserves huge praise.

Ray Stubbs
Sports presenter and former Tranmere Rovers and Bangor
City football player

Former pro footballer, amateur rugby player and full-time sports journalist, Ray has seen it all.

fact file

Former footballer, Ray played for Tranmere Rovers and Bangor City before spending three years as a reporter and presenter with local radio. His move in to TV begin producing shows including A Question of Sport, followed by on-screen reporting duties for 'Match of the Day' and 'Grandstand' and then covering Ireland's campaign at the 1994 FIFA World Cup in America. After over 26 years with the BBC, the veteran football, snooker and darts presenter joined ESPN in 2009 to present Premier League football. In 2007 he missed the Semis of Comic Relief Does Fame Academy as a bad dose of flu hit his singing voice.

Get angry

Some say 'don't get angry, get even', but if getting angry helps yo
to get even it's worth doing from time to time. If you do it too ofter
though, your teammates will see through it.

Louis,

At half-time in the 2005 European Cup Final, some Liverpool fans
were coming up to journalists like myself in the Istanbul press box and
saying that it was time to go home. Liverpool were being outclassed
by AC Milan in the first half, were trailing 3–0 and had only pride to
play for. But Mission Impossible became the Great Escape.

What we did not realise was that down below us, in the Liverpool
dressing-room, a captain was going to work. Steven Gerrard had
heard a passionate speech by his manager, Rafa Benitz, about how
they had to play for the fans, and then the skipper himself spoke a
lively few words. Gerrard was angered by Liverpool's performance,
and the gloating of one or two Milan players, so he launched into
a speech designed to stir his team into life. It worked. Liverpool
tore into Milan in the second half, with Gerrard leading by example,
scoring one, winning the penalty for the second, seeing Liverpool
equalise and then putting in some amazing tackles during extra time,
despite cramp turning his legs to stone. It was one of the greatest
contributions by a captain in the history of the European Cup.

Gerrard's reward for refusing to surrender? He ended up with the
European Cup in his bedroom that night. Life does not get much
better!

Henry Winter
Football correspondent for the *Daily Telegraph* and writer

The most knowledgeable of football correspondents, Henry is first to tweet the very latest news.

fact file

Henry is the award-winning football correspondent for the *Daily Telegraph*, appearing on numerous radio and TV sports programmes, where his insight and up to the minute briefings are keenly sought. Henry has ghostwritten the autobiographies of famous footballers, past and present and co-wrote 'FA Confidential' with David Davies, former FA Chief Executive. With more than 100,000 followers on Twitter, he's the font of knowledge for all things football.

Once more unto the breach

A rousing speech by the captain can pump a team up just before they leave the changing room. It doesn't need to be too complicated. Keep the message simple but say it with passion.

Louis,

I once played at Esher RFC with a guy called Paul Stevens, and his last words before leaving the dressing-room were always: 'There's no point starting a job if you don't intend to finish it.' It didn't really mean much, but it's maybe a good idea always having something 'inspiring' to say before you take to the field.

Also, always remember to lead by example.

John Inverdale
Sports presenter, BBC

Broadcaster John stays warm during the O2 Scrum in the Park event, 2004.

fact file

John played rugby for Devonport Services RFC in his hometown of Plymouth and captained the University of Southampton tennis team before moving into journalism, joining BBC Radio Lincolnshire in 1982. As an award-winning journalist and now one of the best known sports presenters on TV, John made the headlines himself in 200? appearing on screen with a few facial battle scars, the result of his continued love for the game of rugby union, having turned out for Esher RFC. John is also a Lincoln City Football Club fan.

Mr Motivator

A good captain should be always looking to improve 'team spirit' and encouraging each teammate to play with a positive attitude. His or her optimism and confidence must shine through so the team believes they can win.

Louis,

The main skill for a captain is the art of people management – he or she has to motivate their players to get the best out of each one.

Much of the time a captain can lead by example and earn the respect of the players, but it's also important to enjoy the game!

Jonathan Davies MBE
Wales, Neath and Llanelli
rugby union captain

Jonathan in action in Wales' 28-6 win over Western Samoa at Cardiff Arms Park, 1988.

fact file

Initially rejected by Llanelli RFC, the great fly-half signed with Neath RFC in 1982. After 35 games, Jonathan was selected to play for Wales, when he scored a try and a drop goal on his debut against England. He was also named Man of the Match at home in the Cardiff Arms Park. Jonathan played an important part in the 1988 Triple Crown success for Wales and between 1985 and 1997 he won 37 rugby union caps. He was made captain at Neath before joining Llanelli, and he captained Wales on the 1988 New Zealand Tour. In 1989, Jonathan changed codes, moving north to join Widnes Vikings RLFC. In 1995, in the new rugby union professional era, he switched back again and finished his career with Cardiff RFC two years later. Jonathan now commentates for the BBC.

Inspire

Genius, they say, is one per cent inspiration and ninety-nine per cent perspiration. As a sporting captain, you need both.

Louis,

You've obviously been chosen to be captain for various reasons. I'm guessing it will have to be for your playing ability and leadership qualities, so why change?

It's important to keep up your consistency in playing performance, inspire your teammates and, if you can, also help them along the way.

If you can do those three things, you won't go far wrong!

Mark Lawrenson
Republic of Ireland
and Liverpool football

Mark in action against Newcastle St James' Park, 1998.

fact file

Mark began playing football for his home town team – Preston North End – and was their 1976–1977 Player of the Year. He moved to Brighton and Hove Albion, then to Liverpool in 1981 on a then-club-record transfer fee. Mark gained his first of 39 international caps for the Republic of Ireland when he was 19. He is now a respected commentator on the game on TV and radio.